Erin Pembrey Swan

Land Predators Around the World

Franklin Watts · A Division of Scholastic Inc.
New York · Toronto · London · Auckland · Sydney
New Mexico · New Delhi · Hong Kong
Danbury, Connecticut

For Lea,

who made all this possible

Photographs ©: Animals Animals: 25 (Bruce Davidson), 33 (Robert Maier), 5 bottom right (J&B Photographers); ENP Images: 5 bottom left (Gerry Ellis); National Geographic Image Collection: 42 (Raymond K. Gehman); Peter Arnold Inc.: 37 (Gunter Ziesler); Photo Researchers, NY: 35 (Tim Davis), 5 top right (Nigel J. Dennis), 39 (Mark Newman), 17 (M. Reardon), 41 (Jany Sauvanet), 23 (Terry Whittaker), 1, 31 (Art Wolfe); Stock Boston: 43 (Matthew Neal McVay); Stone: 20, 21 (J. Sneesby/B. Wilkins), 18, 19 (Daniel J. Cox), 7 (Tim Davis), 6 (Peter/Stef Lamberti), 12, 13 (S. Purdy Matthews) 15 (Bryan Mullennix); Visuals Unlimited: 28, 29 (Cheryl A. Ertelt), cover, 5 top left, 27 (Joe McDonald).

Illustrations by Jose Gonzales and Steve Savage

The photo on the cover shows a tiger running. The photo on the title page shows two silver-backed jackals.

Library of Congress Cataloging-in-Publication Data

Swan, Erin Pembrey.
Land predators around the world / Erin Pembrey Swan.
     p. cm. — (Animals in order)
     Includes bibliographical references and index.
     Summary: Describes the physical characteristics and behavior of a variety of meat-eating animals, including lions, tigers, cheetahs, jackals, mongooses, meerkats, hyenas, and bears.
     ISBN 0-531-11627-1 (lib. bdg.)
1.   Carnivora—Juvenile literature. [1. Carnivores.] I. Title. II. Series.
QL737.C2 S92 2001
599.7—dc21   99-059418

GROLIER
PUBLISHING   1 2 3 4 5 6 7 8 9 10 R 10 09 08 07 06 05 04 03 02 01

Contents

What Is a Land Predator?

Have you ever watched a cat catch a mouse? Belly to the ground, it creeps slowly toward its unsuspecting prey—slowly, slowly, closer, and closer. The cat wriggles its rear end and tenses its muscles, and then POUNCE! It grabs the mouse with its long, sharp claws.

A house cat is one kind of land *predator*. Although most cats get fed by humans and do not have to search for food, many hunt anyway. Dogs are also land predators. Have you ever seen a dog chase a rabbit? Cats and dogs are the only common household pets that are land predators. There are many others that live and hunt in the wild.

Land predators are *mammals* that kill and eat other animals to survive. These hunters belong to a group, or *order*, called *carnivora* (car-NIV-or-a), which means "flesh-eaters." Although many land predators eat things other than meat, they are natural-born hunters.

Three of the four animals shown on the next page are land predators. Can you tell which one is not?

Porcupine

Meerkat

Coatimundi

Honey badger

Traits of a Land Predator

Did you pick the porcupine? You were right! How could you tell it is not a land predator?

Land predators hunt other animals for food, so they need to have built-in "weapons." Most have sharp teeth and claws. A porcupine has 2 long, square front teeth that are perfect for gnawing the bark and plants it loves to eat. A porcupine's teeth won't help it attack a rabbit, though.

Lions, jackals, hyenas, and other land predators use their teeth to kill prey and tear it apart. Their *canine teeth* are long, large, and pointed. These fanglike teeth help the predator keep a tight grip on its victim until the helpless animal dies. The predator then uses these sharp teeth to carry the prey to a safe eating place. Most land predators have 2 pairs of *carnassial teeth*—composed of interlocking teeth in the upper and lower jaw—made

Can you find this cheetah's canine teeth?

A hyena and two pups

especially for slicing or cutting meat from their victim's bodies. Carnassial teeth are like a built-in knife and fork.

Many land predators also have very sharp claws. The claws of most cats are *retractile*. This means they can be pulled into the paw to make it soft and gentle or pushed out to transform the paw into a dangerous weapon. Retractile claws stay very sharp because they are not dulled as the animal walks and runs. Other land predators have sharp claws, but they are not retractile and are not generally used during hunting.

All land predators have an excellent sense of smell, sharp eyesight, and sensitive hearing. They are usually strong and very fast. All these traits help them hunt for food. Most land predators hunt alone or in pairs, but some, such as lions, hunt in groups.

Land predators may give birth to several babies at one time. These groups of tiny, blind young are called *litters*. The young quickly grow into a furry bunch of eager hunters.

The Order of Living Things

A tiger has more in common with a house cat than with a daisy. A true bug is more like a butterfly than a jellyfish. Scientists arrange living things into groups based on how they look and how they act. A tiger and a house cat belong to the same group, but a daisy belongs to a different group.

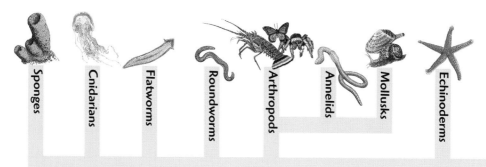

Sponges | Cnidarians | Flatworms | Roundworms | Arthropods | Annelids | Mollusks | Echinoderms

Animals

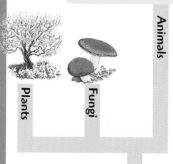

Plants | Fungi

Monerans | Protists

All living things can be placed in one of five groups called *kingdoms*: the plant kingdom, the animal kingdom, the fungus kingdom, the moneran kingdom, or the protist kingdom. You can probably name many of the creatures in the plant and animal kingdoms. The fungus kingdom includes mushrooms, yeasts, and mold. The moneran and protist kingdoms contain thousands of living things that are too small to see without a microscope.

8

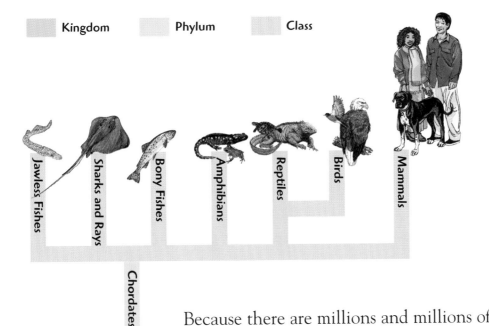

Kingdom   **Phylum**   **Class**

Jawless Fishes

Sharks and Rays

Bony Fishes

Amphibians

Reptiles

Birds

Mammals

Chordates

Because there are millions and millions of living things on Earth, some of the members of one kingdom may not seem all that similar. The animal kingdom includes creatures as different as tarantulas and trout, jellyfish and jaguars, salamanders and sparrows, elephants and earthworms.

To show that an elephant is more like a jaguar than an earthworm, scientists further separate the creatures in each kingdom into more specific groups. The animal kingdom can be divided into nine *phyla*. Humans belong to the chordate phylum. All chordates have a backbone.

Each phylum can be subdivided into many *classes*. Humans, mice, and elephants all belong to the mammal class. Each class can be further divided into orders; orders into *families*, families into *genera*, and genera into *species*. All the members of a species are very similar.

9

How Land Predators Fit In

You can probably guess that the land predators belong to the animal kingdom. They have much more in common with bees and bats than with maple trees and morning glories.

Land predators belong to the chordate phylum. Almost all chordates have a backbone and a skeleton. Can you think of other chordates? Examples include zebras, mice, snakes, birds, fish, and whales.

The chordate phylum can be divided into a number of classes. Land predators belong to the mammal class. Mice, whales, dogs, cats, and humans are all mammals.

There are seventeen different orders of mammals. The land predators make up one of these orders. As you learned earlier, all land predators have features that help them capture, kill, and eat other animals.

The land predators can be divided into a number of different families and genera, and many different species. Land predators live in all kinds of *habitats* and on every continent except Antarctica. In this book, you will learn more about fifteen species of land predators that live in different parts of the world.

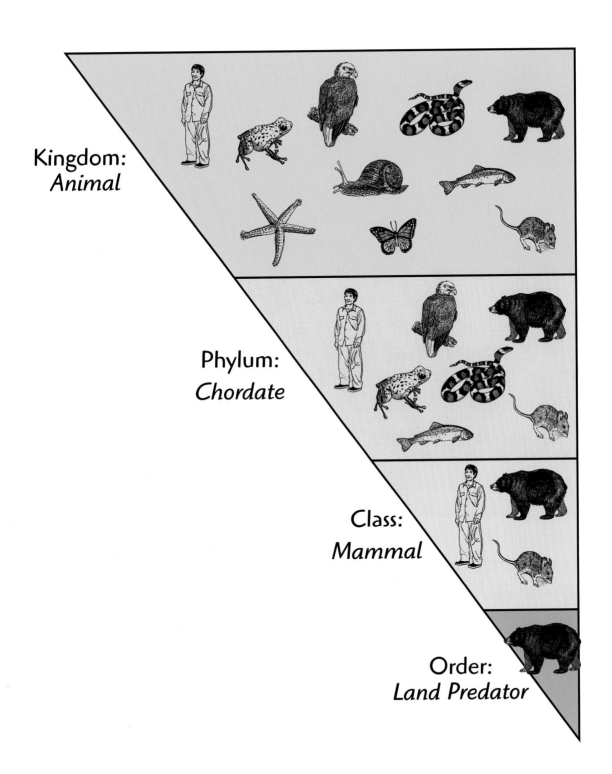

Kingdom:
Animal

Phylum:
Chordate

Class:
Mammal

Order:
Land Predator

11

Lions

FAMILY: Felidae
COMMON EXAMPLE: African lion
GENUS AND SPECIES: *Panthera leo*
SIZE: 60 to 72 inches (152 to 183 cm)

In the cool evening, a group of lionesses slink through the long, dry grass in a plain. Bellies to the ground, they creep slowly toward a herd of wildebeest grazing nearby. They see a young calf standing slightly apart from the herd, and the lionesses fan out to form a circle around the calf. Then one lioness springs forward and leaps onto the calf. She lands on its back, sinks her teeth into its neck, and knocks it to the ground. The other lionesses close in on the helpless calf.

Lions live together in large family groups called *prides*. After a kill, full-grown lions and lionesses eat first. Cubs and weaker lions hang back and wait their turn. Hyenas, too, prowl around and watch for a chance to dart in and steal the kill.

Lions rest near shady water holes during long, hot days. In the evening, the lionesses go off to hunt while the males guard the *territory*.

12

Although females stay in their prides all their lives, males are kicked out when they are adults. They wander and hunt alone until they find a new pride to join. They have to fight other males to join the group. Most prides have 1 or 2 males with a number of adult females and their cubs. Lions are the only species of cats that live in groups.

Meerkats

FAMILY: Viverridae

COMMON NAME: Meerkat

GENUS AND SPECIES: *Suricata suricatta*

SIZE: 20 inches (51 cm)

Three meerkats sit upright on their hind legs and bask in the warm sun on a southern African plain. One reason these small predators sit upright is to watch for their many enemies. At the first sign of a hungry eagle or jackal, a meerkat whistles shrilly to alert other members of its group. Then all of them dive quickly into their safe *burrows*.

These long, slender creatures spend the night sleeping in the huge network of burrows that they dig in the sandy soil. In the morning, they come out to hunt, play, and care for their young. During the wet season, when it is very hot, they take afternoon naps to escape from the heat.

Meerkats like to be together. They live in groups numbering from 5 to 40. They take turns with their work. While some meerkats hunt, others stay behind to babysit or keep watch for danger.

Meerkats will eat almost anything—from beetles to lizards. They even catch and eat scorpions and poisonous snakes. Like their relatives, the mongooses, venom doesn't seem to bother them.

Zorillas

FAMILY: Mustelidae
COMMON NAME: Zorilla
GENUS AND SPECIES: *Ictonyx striatus*
SIZE: 13 to 15 inches (33 to 38 cm)

A zorilla pokes its snout out of its burrow and sniffs the evening air. Mmm! It smells many tasty creatures, from plump frogs to juicy mice. This zorilla has spent the long, hot day resting in its cool burrow, and now it is hungry and ready to hunt. It shuffles out of its hole and waddles off across the plain as it looks for a crunchy insect or a tasty snake.

These furry, short-legged predators look like skunks, their North American relatives. Like skunks, zorillas have a clever way to defend themselves from enemies. If a zorilla is attacked, it will usually play dead until its attacker gets bored and leaves. But if that doesn't work, the zorilla squirts a foul-smelling liquid from glands under its tail. The liquid burns the attacker's eyes. It will be a long time before that enemy attacks another zorilla!

Zorillas live in Africa, mostly in open grassland and brushy plains. They live alone, except when mothers raise their young. Zorillas meet only during mating season. After the zorillas mate, they part again. About 1 month later, the females give birth in their burrows or under rocks, where their young can grow up safe from danger.

Cheetahs

FAMILY: Felidae
COMMON NAME: Cheetah
GENUS AND SPECIES: *Acinonyx jubatus*
SIZE: 44 to 59 inches (112 to 150 cm)

Watch out, gazelle! A cheetah dashes out of the long grass and sprints toward its prey. The gazelle tries to run, but it's too late. The super-fast cheetah catches it and knocks it to the ground with a sharp-clawed paw. With one expert bite, the cheetah sinks its teeth into the gazelle's throat and holds it until it suffocates. The struggle is over. The tired cheetah drags its kill off to a shady spot and begins to eat.

Cheetahs are the fastest land mammals in the world. They can run up to 70 miles per hour (113 kmh) for short distances, but they usually chase their prey at half that speed to save energy. They tire easily, too, so they have to catch a fleeing gazelle or impala quickly. Otherwise, they slow down, and the animal gets away.

These quick, spotted predators live on the Serengeti plains and in northern Iran. When cheetahs are not hunting, they perch on fallen trees or

18

on termite mounds. There, they bask in the sun and scan the plains for prey.

Although most adult cheetahs live and hunt alone, mothers and cubs are very close. A mother cheetah will fiercely defend her small, furry cubs from any predators, including hungry hyenas. With her sharp teeth and claws, she can scare away just about any animal!

Honey Badgers

FAMILY: Mustelidae
COMMON NAME: Honey badger
GENUS AND SPECIES: *Mellivora capensis*
SIZE: 24 to 30 inches (61 to 76 cm)

Follow me! A honey guide bird flies in front of a honey badger and leads it straight to a beehive. With its powerful legs and strong claws, the honey badger tears into the hive, exposing a tasty mess of honey. It drives the bees away with a smelly liquid that comes from glands under its tail. Then it pokes its snout in the honey and begins to eat. When the honey badger is done, there is still some honey left for the patient honey guide bird. The bird finally gets its reward for finding the hive. Now that's cooperation!

Although honey is a honey badger's favorite treat, it has a varied diet—from berries and eggs to insects and mice. Sometimes a honey badger will eat animals that are already dead, but this stocky, muscular predator is strong enough to kill a young wildebeest or a waterbuck. Some honey badgers have driven lions away from their kills!

Honey badgers live mostly in Africa, but some are found in Asia. In these places, they can live in almost any habitat as long as it isn't too wet or too dry. Honey badgers wander alone or in pairs and roam a wide territory in search of food. They sleep in shallow burrows, but they rarely stay there more than one night. They prefer to travel from one burrow to another as they search for food.

Mongooses

FAMILY: Viverridae
COMMON EXAMPLE: Marsh mongoose
GENUS AND SPECIES: *Atilax paludinosus*
SIZE: 12 to 16 inches (30 to 41 cm)

A marsh mongoose stands near the bank in a shallow river. Holding its head out of the water, it sifts patiently through the mud and water with its front paws. Aha! What's this? With one quick motion, the mongoose pulls out a freshwater crab and hurls it against a rock. Crack! The crab's hard shell breaks open, revealing the juicy meat inside. A perfect meal for a hungry mongoose!

Although crabs, mussels, and snails are marsh mongooses' favorite foods, they will eat almost anything. A mongoose can make a tasty meal out of a fat, juicy frog or a crunchy insect.

These predators live in African swamps. They follow pathways along rivers and lakeshores as they hunt for food. Tall grass and reeds hide marsh mongooses from their prey. They often slip into the water, where they find most of their food.

Marsh mongooses like to live alone. They mark their swampy homes with scent from their glands. If a mongoose is attacked, it growls and barks sharply and shows its sharp teeth. If it is cornered, it sprays its attacker with a nasty brown fluid that comes from glands under its tail. The fluid's strong, horrible smell says, "Keep away!"

Jackals

FAMILY: Canidae
COMMON EXAMPLE: Black-backed jackal
GENUS AND SPECIES: *Canis mesomelas*
SIZE: 28 inches (71 cm)

After a hunt, a mother jackal trots back to her cubs with her belly full. The 2-week-old cubs crowd around her hungrily. With a special, practiced motion, she brings the half-digested meat up out of her stomach. Now the meat is soft enough for the tiny pups to chew, and they devour it quickly.

At 3 months, jackal pups are old enough to tag along on hunting trips. Soon they are big enough to hunt on their own, but most of them don't. Young jackals usually stay with their parents for 1 or 2 years to help raise the next litter. Jackals make great baby-sitters. They tend the young while other adults roam the plains in search of food. If strange jackals come near, they chase them off with barks and growls.

Black-backed jackals live in the African grassland. They usually mate for life. The mated jackals go almost everywhere together. At sunrise and sunset, they prowl the plains for food. Although they hunt alone for smaller prey such as mice and lizards, it takes at least 2 jackals to bring down a young gazelle. Then the jackals feed. Soon the hungry little pups waiting back at the *den* will have their share!

Tigers

FAMILY: Felidae
COMMON NAME: Tiger
GENUS AND SPECIES: *Panthera tigris*
SIZE: 60 to 70 inches (152 to 178 cm)

A tiger rests in the cool, flickering shade of a mangrove swamp. Its striped coat, unique as a human fingerprint, blends with the shadows and hides the tiger from view. As dusk approaches, it rises to its feet and stretches. After the hot tropical day, this tiger is very hungry. It slips quietly from its dense cover and pads off through the trees in search of food.

Except for a mother with cubs, tigers live and hunt alone. Although they will eat anything they can catch, they like big game best. To catch a deer or another large animal, a tiger creeps silently through the underbrush. When it's close enough to attack, the tiger dashes out, springs at the deer, and knocks it to the ground. One long, deep bite to the throat, and the victim is dead. The tiger now has enough food for a few days. It stays close to its kill and eats a little every day until it's gone.

Tigers live anywhere with dense cover for hunting—from tropical rain forests to mangrove swamps. Although tigers are land predators, they stay close to water. They

are strong swimmers, and they like to bathe in rivers and lakes when they are hot.

Each tiger has its own territory that it marks with urine. A male's territory often overlaps that of several females. They meet during mating season. The tigers rub heads and make a puffing sound. In tiger language, this sound means, "Hello, who are you?"

Binturongs

FAMILY: Viverridae
COMMON NAME: Binturong
GENUS AND SPECIES: *Arctictis binturong*
SIZE: 24 to 36 inches (61 to 91 cm)

Whose whiskery face is peering through the leaves? It's a binturong sniffing the air for food. Yum! It smells a cluster of juicy figs on the next tree. Hungrily but slowly, the binturong moves through the branches toward the figs.

Binturongs are furry creatures that live in the forests of Southeast Asia. Awkward on the ground, they spend most of their time in trees. Up there, they find most of their food. Although they like fruit best, they eat birds, mice, and other small animals too.

During the day, a binturong rests in tree branches. When night falls, it is ready to hunt. As the binturong creeps through the trees, it rubs oil from glands under its tail onto the branches. This tells other binturongs, "I was here."

A binturong's long, flexible tail is special. Fully *prehensile*, the tail grips branches and keeps the binturong from falling as it clambers along high in the treetops. When a binturong reaches for food with its front feet, it steadies itself by gripping a branch with its tail. When a binturong sits up, it balances on its hind legs and tail like a kangaroo. What would a binturong do without its tail?

Marbled Polecats

FAMILY: Mustelidae
COMMON NAME: Marbled polecat
GENUS AND SPECIES: *Vormela peregusna*
SIZE: 11 to 14 inches (28 to 36 cm)

A marbled polecat sniffs the opening of an underground tunnel. With its sharp sense of smell, the polecat picks up the scent of rabbit. Stomach growling, it slips into the tunnel in search of its prey. With their long, slender bodies, polecats can fit easily into the narrow openings of rabbit burrows. The smaller females can even squirm down into the burrows of rats and voles. This is the perfect way for hungry polecats to catch food.

Marbled polecats are relatives of the weasel. They live in the dry, grassy plains of Europe and Asia. During the day, they curl up to sleep in underground nests. In the early evening, they come out to hunt. They feast on almost anything—from mice and rabbits to lizards and frogs. If polecats catch more than they can eat, they hide their food in a burrow. The next time they get hungry, the leftovers make a great snack!

Each polecat has its own territory, which it defends fiercely. If a fox or another enemy attacks, a polecat fluffs its fur, bares its teeth, and growls. If that isn't enough to scare its enemy, the polecat turns around and squirts out a stinky liquid from glands under its tail.

Bears

FAMILY: Ursidae
COMMON NAME: Brown bear
GENUS AND SPECIES: *Ursus arctos*
SIZE: 59 to 110 inches (150 to 280 cm)

It is summer, and a bulky, shaggy brown bear sits by a bush. The bear delicately plucks off berries with its rubbery lips and long tongue. When the berries are gone, the bear is still hungry. It ambles off in search of a juicy plant root or some yummy mushrooms.

With their heavy, clawed paws and sharp teeth, brown bears also catch mice, ground squirrels, and marmots. When brown bears are really hungry, they will eat dead animals. They can smell them from up to 2 miles (3 km) away!

These heavy, flat-footed predators rest during the day and search for food in the evening or early morning. Bears who live where the winters are cold curl up in snug dens when the first snow falls. They sleep through most of the winter and live on stored fat. In spring, they come out yawning, stretching, and feeling very hungry.

Brown bears live in small numbers across Europe and in Asia, including Siberia and the Himalayas. These predators also live in northwestern North America. Although brown bears usually live alone, mothers with cubs form a very close family. Brown bears are rarely dangerous, but don't ever get between a mother and her cubs. A mother brown bear fiercely protects her young.

Coatimundis

FAMILY: Procyonidae
COMMON EXAMPLE: Ring-tailed coatimundi
GENUS AND SPECIES: *Nasua nasua*
SIZE: 24 inches (61 cm)

What is making all that noise? It's a ring-tailed coatimundi looking for food. Shuffling through the forest, it pokes its long snout into holes and cracks as it searches for tasty beetles. Snorting and snuffling, the ring-tailed coatimundi rustles through fallen leaves and searches for centipedes, worms, and ants. This land predator tears into rotting logs with its sharp claws to uncover termites. Then it quickly snaps them up and swallows them.

Although ring-tailed coatimundis like insects best, they eat rodents, lizards, and fruit too. Their bodies are well adapted for hunting. When coatimundis climb trees to find food, they use their tails to balance on slender branches. Their ankles are so flexible that their feet can turn around completely. With this special skill, they can climb down trees headfirst. You won't find a ring-tailed coatimundi stuck helplessly in a tree!

These small, ring-tailed predators live in the forests of Central and South America. Although males wander alone, females and their young live together in groups of 4 to 20. They sleep at night in treetop nests made of branches and leaves. During the day, they wander the forest as they hunt, rest, and groom each other.

If ring-tailed coatimundis are attacked, the entire group will leap into the trees. Loud woofs and clicking sounds tell the intruder, "Go away!"

Ocelots

FAMILY: Felidae
COMMON NAME: Ocelot
GENUS AND SPECIES: *Felis pardalis*
SIZE: 40 inches (102 cm)

It is nighttime in the South American jungle. A slender, spotted ocelot creeps along the ground as it eyes a young peccary nearby. Slowly the ocelot crawls closer. Then, with a sudden dash and a spring, it leaps onto the peccary and brings it to the ground. The fight is soon over. The ocelot will eat well tonight.

Ocelots are small, secretive cats that live from southwestern Texas to northern Argentina. They live anywhere with dense cover—jungles, mountains, and plains. Ocelots sleep alone during the day and hunt alone at night. They meet only during mating season. After the ocelets mate, they part again. The kittens that are born 2 to 3 months later keep their mother company for a little while. The kittens wander off to find their own homes when they are around 1 year old.

Both males and females have their own territories that they defend from others. They hunt within their territory. Ocelots have a varied diet. They eat mammals such as rabbits, monkeys, and small anteaters, but they will hunt iguanas, frogs, and crabs too. Sometimes they even climb trees to snag an unlucky bird.

Kinkajous

FAMILY: Procyonidae
COMMON NAME: Kinkajou
GENUS AND SPECIES: *Potus flavus*
SIZE: 17 to 22 inches (43 to 56 cm)

A kinkajou wraps its long tail around a tree branch, digs in with its hind claws, and lets its front feet swing free. Now it can reach that plump fig hanging nearby. It's a good thing its tail is so strong. It's a long way down to the ground!

Kinkajous are furry, golden-brown relatives of the raccoon. They live in forests from Mexico to South America. Kinkajous stay high in the trees and hardly ever climb down to the ground. They have everything they need in the trees.

These land predators sleep during the day in shady tree hollows and awaken in the evening to hunt. Sometimes kinkajous catch tree frogs and crunch on insects, but kinkajous really like fruit best—especially figs and bananas. When kinkajous eat, they turn on their sides or backs so no fruit juice will trickle away. Kinkajous love flower nectar too. They lap it up with their long tongues.

Kinkajous live alone and mark their territories with scent from their glands. They meet only when they mate and raise young. But if a tree is especially full of fruit, kinkajous will gather to feed. They bark and growl as they eat, fighting over the fattest fig or the ripest banana.

Land Predators and People

Did you know that lions used to live in Greece and cheetahs once roamed through India? Tigers lived throughout Asia many years ago, but now there are fewer than 5,000 left in the wild. Some tigers, such as the Caspian and the Balinese, may even be gone completely. Where have all these predators gone?

One reason that some predators are threatened or endangered is that people have hunted them. Farmers and ranchers have shot many land predators to protect their livestock. Cheetahs and ocelots were killed for their beautiful spotted coats. People killed binturongs and sold some of their body parts for food and others for medicine. Bears, tigers, and lions all were hunted for sport. Many people thought a stuffed bear or a tiger pelt made an excellent trophy. Now there are fewer land predators.

These hunters have killed a bear.

Predators and other animals are also in danger because people destroy their homes. When people build cities, roads, housing developments, shopping centers, and factories, many land predators lose their habitats. In many places, it's hard for animals to find a wide plain or a thick, safe forest in which to live. Sometimes there are open fields, but people till them or let animals graze there. These activities also harm the habitats of wild animals.

People are trying to protect land predators and preserve their habitats. Laws have been passed to protect these animals. National parks and wildlife refuges provide protected areas for many animals.

However, many people still hunt land predators illegally because their fur and other body parts can be sold for a lot of money. Wild animals are still losing their habitats. Much more work needs to be done to save them. Can you think of a way to protect predators?

Wildlife agents show illegal products made from land predators.

43

Words to Know

burrow—a shelter dug in the ground

canine teeth—pointed teeth that land predators use to catch and hold their prey

carnassial teeth—teeth behind the canine teeth that land predators use to slice or cut meat

carnivora—the name for the order of flesh-eating mammals

class—a group of creatures within a phylum that share certain characteristics

den—the shelter or resting place of a wild animal

family—a group of creatures within an order that share certain characteristics

genus (plural genera)—a group of creatures within a family that share certain characteristics

habitat—the environment where a plant or animal lives and grows

kingdom—one of the five divisions into which all living things are placed: the animal kingdom, the plant kingdom, the fungus kingdom, the moneran kingdom, and the protist kingdom

litter—the name for a group of newborn land predators

mammal—an animal that has a backbone and drinks mother's milk when it is young

order—a group of creatures within a class that share certain characteristics

phylum (plural **phyla**)—a group of creatures within a kingdom that share certain characteristics

predator—an animal that hunts and eats other animals

prehensile tail—a tail that can grasp like a hand

pride—the name for a group of lions

retractile claws—claws of some land predators that can be pulled back into the paw

species—a group of creatures within a genus that share certain characteristics. Members of the same species can mate and produce healthy young.

territory—the area of land that an animal claims as its own and defends against rivals

Learning More

Books

Collard, Sneed B., III. *Tough Terminators: Twelve of the Earth's Most Fascinating Predators*. Minocqua, WI: Northword Press, 1994.

Discovery Communications. *Who's for Dinner? Predators and Prey*. New York: Crown Publishers, 1998.

Lumpkin, Susan. *Big Cats*. New York: Facts On File, 1993.

Pringle, Laurence. *Jackal Woman: Exploring the World of Jackals*. New York: Atheneum, 1993.

Videos

Carnivores. Bill Burrud's Amazing Animal World.

Predators of the Wild. Time Warner Home Video.

Web Sites

5 Tigers: The Tiger Information Center

http://www.5tigers.org/

This site discusses the five tiger subspecies and why they are endangered. There is an "Adventures" link that includes fun games involving tigers.

Bears and Other Top Predators

http://www.bearsmag.com/

This magazine's site includes articles about bears and other predators from current and past issues, a photo gallery, and links.

Index

About the Author

Erin Pembrey Swan studied animal behavior, literature, and early childhood education at Hampshire College in Massachusetts. She also studied literature and history at University College Galway in Ireland. Her poetry has been published in *The Poet's Gallery: The Subterraneans* and *The Poet's Gallery: Voices of Selene* in Woodstock, New York, and *The Cuirt Journal* in Galway, Ireland. Ms. Swan is also the author of *Primates: From Howler Monkeys to Humans*, *Land Predators of North America*, *Camels and Pigs: What They Have in Common*, and *Kangaroos and Koalas: What They Have in Common*. Although she lives in New York City, Ms. Swan spends a great deal of time traveling.